Two Bears
go fishing

Story by Cathie and David Bell

Pictures by Jan Brychta

Oxford University Press

For Emily

Oxford University Press, Walton Street, Oxford OX2 6DP

Oxford   New York   Toronto
Delhi   Bombay   Calcutta   Madras   Karachi
Petaling Jaya   Singapore   Hong Kong   Tokyo
Nairobi   Dar es Salaam   Cape Town
Melbourne   Auckland

and associated companies in
Berlin   Ibadan

Oxford is a trade mark of Oxford University Press

© Oxford University Press 1990
Printed in Hong Kong

A CIP catalogue record for this book is available from the British Library.

The Two Bears Books are:

Two Bears at the seaside
Two Bears in the snow
Two Bears at the party
Two Bears go fishing
Two Bears find a pet
Two Bears and the fireworks

One day, Winston woke up early.
He looked out of the window.
'Wake up, Stanley,' he shouted.
'It's a lovely day to go fishing.
You make a picnic and I'll get dressed.'

Stanley went downstairs and packed the picnic basket while Winston put on his red bow tie and a straw hat.

Stanley took the go-kart out of the shed and then he brought out the picnic basket.
It was very heavy!

Winston sat on the basket and Stanley drove.
They went down the hill.

The go-kart was too heavy.
It went faster and faster.

Then a terrible thing happened!
The go-kart went over a bump and Winston fell off!
But Stanley and the picnic basket kept on going,
down to the bottom of the hill.

It took Winston a long time to walk down the hill.
'I'm worn out. I'd better just sit here and look after the picnic,' he puffed, 'while you do the fishing.'

Stanley was very good at fishing.
He stood in the water and kept very still.
The fish swam happily around his legs.

Then, quick as a flash,
Stanley reached down into the water and
grabbed a slippery little fish with his paws!

Every time Stanley caught one more fish,
Winston cheered loudly and had one more sandwich.

By the end of the morning, Stanley had caught ten fish, and Winston had eaten ten sandwiches.

Stanley made a big fire to cook the fish.
When everything was ready, Winston took out a match and lit the fire.

When the fish were cooked, Winston and Stanley ate them on sticks. They were delicious!

Then they put everything away in the basket
and sat watching the fire glowing.
'I love fishing,' said Winston.
'Let's do it again tomorrow!' said Stanley.
And they did!